theworkingsinglemom.com's Field Guide to Changing the Game... for 2020

FIRST EDITION

© 2019 by Noelle Federico

All rights reserved. No part of this book may be reproduced without the permission in writing from the author, except by a reviewer who may quote brief passages in a review with appropriate credit; nor may any part of this book be reproduced, stored in a retrieval system, or transmitted in any form or by any means-electronic, photocopying, recording or other- without permission in writing from the publisher.

For information or permissions write:

One11 Publishing
Hendersonville, TN

www.one11publishing.com
One11 Publishing is an imprint of
Newbern Consulting, LLC

Publisher: Sedrik Newbern, Newbern Consulting, LLC
Cover Design by Creative Pear www.creativepear.net
Back Cover Photo by Tia Rooney Photography, Fairfax, VT

ISBN Paperback: 978-1-7329512-9-7
Library of Congress Control Number: 2019915861

"Each time he said,
'My GRACE is all you need.
My POWER works best in weakness.'

So now I am glad to boast about
My weaknesses, so that the power
of Christ can work through me."

2 Corinthians 12:9 (NLT)

DEDICATION

To GOD goes the all the Glory… He continues to make ways where there are no ways, and my life is a living testimony of His power and Grace.

To my son Antonio, my greatest work, my greatest lesson and my greatest love… you are truly my finest contribution to the planet… I love you to the moon and back buggy.

To John and to Mark… that I am blessed enough to spend the second half of my life here living with one of you and working for the other makes every single thing that I have suffered in the first half worth it… I would do it all again as long as the story ended with the two of you by my side. Whop you had me at "hi" 20 years ago and Mark you are truly one of the greatest men that I have ever met and I still strive to be you when I grow up. The two of you, each in your own way make every day an amazing gift and I thank you for that from the bottom of my heart. I no longer wake up scared and that I owe to each of you…you both have my heart forever and then for whatever comes after that. Thank you. I love you more. XO

To the followers, supporters and fans of **The Working Single Mom** brand, thank you for allowing me into your lives and thank you for every day pushing me to work harder and do better so that I will have insights to share with you…you are all MY inspiration…keep going, you got this…

*** Sometime in 2016...in my backyard...*

God said to me..." And if I take everything from you, will you TRUST me and stand on what you know?

Or will you forsake me?"

I answered, "I will not forsake you..."

Then the response, "Then let your testimony prove my legacy of good no matter what it looks like..."

And so it began...

INTRODUCTION

If you are new to my work, welcome aboard. If you have been following me through time, welcome back. In 2014, when I created **The Working Single Mom** brand it struck me that I should make a workbook that would help my audience plan for the new year in a way that would make a difference...then life got in the way and I looked up and it was the Summer of 2019! Better late than never and so this workbook became a reality and will shortly be in your hands so that you can use it to have an incredible 2020.

The questions and tools that I present here will only CHANGE the game for you if you USE them and do the work. Change takes work, consistent effort and discipline to go from who you are now to who you wish to be. Truly (and I speak from experience) anything is possible as long as you are willing to do the work. You have to do the work...there is no other way.

If your life is not what you envisioned it to be then it's time to change the game for yourself and get moving on creating habits and behaviors that will manifest the circumstances and conditions that you want instead of the ones you are living in. You can do it. I don't give a shit what your current hellish mess is, you absolutely CAN CHANGE IT. I know this because I did it and I continue to do it—day after day—year after year.

I have been a working single mom for almost 19 years now and when my son was 18 months old I had to file bankruptcy and my car was repossessed and I had nothing---I never took child support and I still managed to figure it out and create an incredible life—if I can do it, you can do it. The ideas, questions and tools included in this workbook are what I used to create the life that I have now, the questions in here are questions that I continually ask myself...there is nothing in this creation of mine that I haven't road tested.

Fire Seasons are what I call those times in your life that you think you cannot survive—the bankruptcy was a Fire Season, moving back to VT in 2015 was a Fire Season and I am just at the tail end of one of my hardest Fire Seasons---about 2.5 years ago I left a very good, high-paying corporate job to go back to full time consulting under my own company, my income was reduced by 75% and my expenses were not. I moved through this last season by standing on the principles that I teach...I stood on them when it did not look like I could pay the mortgage, I stood on them when I was laying on the floor crying because I was so scared about how I would pay for everything, I stood on them when the fear almost kept me from breathing....

I STOOD and I STOOD and I practiced and I STOOD some more, I sold everything that I had worth selling and I STOOD, I prayed and I STOOD, I kept having different ideas about the direction of my company and I STOOD, I had the fear and panic and I STOOD anyway, then just as it looked better a construction truck & trailer crossed the median, destroyed my brand new car and almost killed me and STILL I STOOD—I refused to be moved by what it looked like all around me. I kept working the tools and principles that I have practiced since I was 12. I STOOD and I let the shit storm swarm around me and I bent yet did not break and then it moved, just a tiny bit at first and I was able to breathe—and then it moved some more and some more...and now I still have a bit to go, however it is humming right along.

If I could walk through this Fire Season standing on these principles, so can you. I did the work every day, I still do...I use the lists, the index cards, the affirmations...all of it...I work it and it WORKS. If you work it, it WILL work for you too. Some of you that have been following me for a while can attest to this already, you have put these tools to work for you and you have changed the game.

It's high time that you have the life that you always wanted because if not now, WHEN?

You are worth doing the work to create what you want, so let's get to it.

Much Love,

Noelle

Vermont—Sept. 19, 2019

My intention is that you use the material in this workbook to change the game for yourself…that you answer the questions honestly and that you do the work to create the life that you want for yourself and your family.

Let's start by evaluating 2019 as it closes out…start to think about what happened this year (2019)---what should be celebrated, what you want to leave behind you, the blessings, the lessons…there is an immense amount of power in completion, many times we are so busy just trying to 'get by' that we forget to really LOOK at what happened…so take some time and let's be complete with this year…

What worked in 2019?

What didn't work in 2019?

What got accomplished in 2019?

What did not get accomplished that you thought would?

What were your 5 biggest blessings this year?

What were the 5 major lessons you learned in 2019?

What habits or behaviors do you need to leave behind as you finish off this year?

What attitudes do you want to leave behind in 2019?

What is the MOST significant thing that occurred in 2019? And how do you feel about it?

What is there to be celebrated about this past year?

What do you need to be reminded NOT to repeat in 2020?

Rate 2019 on a scale of 1 to 10--- 10 being the BEST

What word describes/ sums up 2019?

Okay, good work…take one last look over your 2019 wrap-up and then let's bless it ALL…the lessons, the hard stuff, the celebrations…all of it. Now declare yourself complete, forgiving yourself for all the things that you think you could have done better. Accept that you did the best you could, and it was all perfect. Now let's move on to what's next…

There are a few tools/practices that if used consistently will help you change the game for yourself...

1. Learn to RESPOND vs. REACT

    A reaction is based solely on emotion and is usually done in a heated moment whereas a response is something that is measured and considered beforehand. Nothing good or lifechanging is going to come from a reaction...mostly when we are reacting, we are actually reacting to things that have happened in the past and it takes away all of our power. Begin to teach yourself to take a breath and walk away when you are 'reacting' and come back when you are ready with a response that suits the situation.

2. Use the Index Card exercise

    Remember flash cards when you were a kid? We used them to train ourselves to learn information such as our multiplication tables or the periodic table of elements...now we are going to use them to alter the way that you think about your life. Get 10 index cards and on each card write an affirmation or statement of how you want your life to be.

Examples:
- I have $5000.00 in a savings account.
- I am well paid with plenty of money to spare and share.
- I work out daily and eat only foods that serve me.
- My relationships contribute to my life.
- My children are happy and healthy.
- I have plenty of energy to do what needs to be done by me.

You get the idea...once you have your 10 statements then use the cards twice a day, flipping through them until the statements on them are really ingrained in your thinking. Change/update the cards statements as needed.

3. Choose Words Wisely

Your words have a LOT more power than you think they do...stop complaining, stop talking about what you don't want more of, speak about things based on how you want them to be and not on the way that they look in the moment. NEVER judge anything by the way that it looks in the current moment, see the outcome that you want to have happen and start looking at things in this way. You will create what you speak about—so make sure that you are speaking LIFE into situations and not repeating doom and gloom.

4. Bookend Your Days

This is a tool that I learned from reading Darren Hardy's book, *The Compound Effect*, it means to make time each morning and each evening to focus on what IS working and pray or read something inspiring and take control of the day in the way that works for you. I suggest in the morning setting a few intentions for the day and in the evening using a Gratitude Journal to write down at least 5 things that you are grateful for. If you bookend your days, then you are able to set the tone at beginning and end no matter what happens in the middle. As Jim Rohn says, "either you run the day, or the day runs you."

Here are some Daily Sheet Templates that can help you bookend your days:

Revealing Excellence....Daily

"Life is a progress and not a station." -Ralph Waldo Emerson

Revealing Excellence... One Week At A Time

5 EXCELLENCE Goals for the WEEK

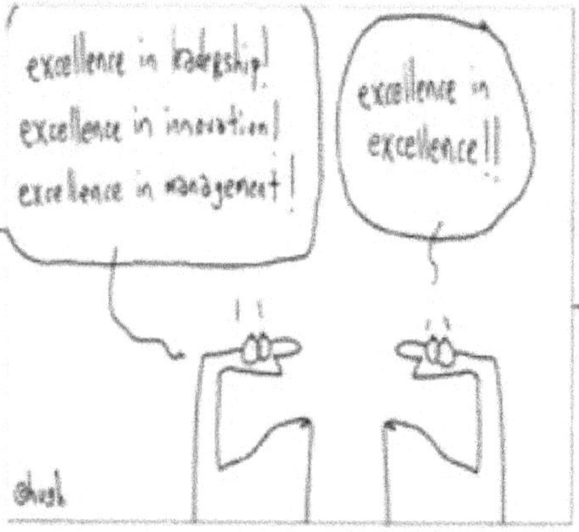

5 EXCELLENCE Goals for the MONTH

5 WOWS for the week

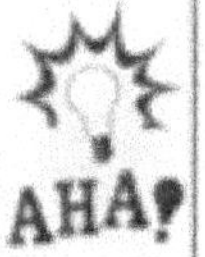

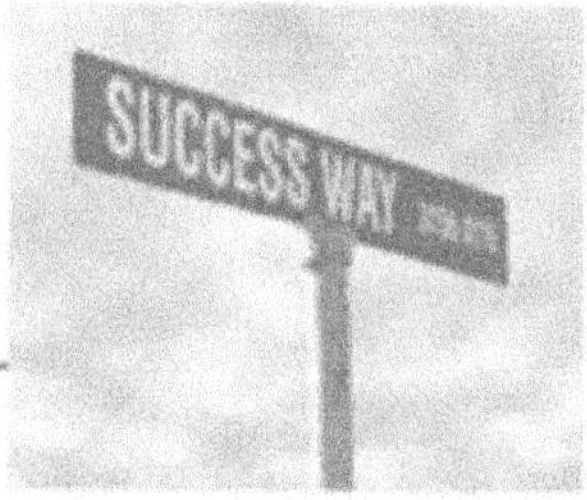

5 Successes during the week

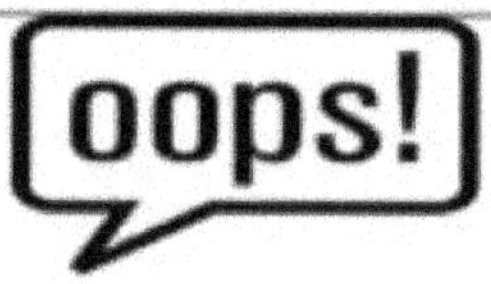

5 oops during the week

"Thousands of geniuses live and die undiscovered— either by themselves or by other."
— Mark Twain

THE DAILY PLAN

Date:

Word for today:

What I want to manifest today:

What I am grateful for today:

Top 3 To Do's

1.
2.
3.

Affirmations for today:

1.
2.

© 2016 Fortunato Partners, Inc., theworkingsinglemom.com ®

5. Be Accountable

Keep your word, walk your talk and own your truth. Don't try to be something that you aren't, be authentic and fearless. You are unique with amazing gifts to offer---**OWN** that shit.

6. Write It Down

Use the listing process... Manifestation list, Gratitude List and Elimination List. You can find them here:

What I Want to MANIFEST...

**This or something better...   © 2018 Fortunato Partners Inc

What I Am GRATEFUL For...

© 2018 Fortunato Partners Inc.

What I Want to ELIMINATE...

(things, behaviors, habits, attitudes, etc...DO NOT put PEOPLE on this list)

© 2018 Fortunato Partners Inc.

7. Picture Your Good

Use Vision Boards or Image Books or Treasure Maps to picture the good that you want to manifest...helping your mind to SEE where you want to go is a powerful tool.

TIME TO CHANGE THE GAME FOR 2020....

What was your total Income in 2019?

What is your income goal for 2020?

What are some side hustle ideas for more revenue streams?

What do you want to read in 2020?

What do you want to watch in 2020?

What do you want to learn? Any classes that you want to take? What seminars do you want to attend?

What have you been directing your attention to?
Is that working?

How are you framing your historic stories? Are you a victim? Is that working?

Given that your health is your most vital asset....
What is your current weight?
What is your goal weight?

What will you do to reach this weight goal in 2020?

What boundaries do you need to establish in 2020 to stay healthy and sane?

Where do you need to start saying NO?

Where can you give back and make a difference this year?

What are the FIVE most important things that you have learned in the last 10 years?

What is the ABSOLUTE best thing about you?

What do you LOVE about yourself right now?

What do you want to change this year?

In 5 years how do you want your life to look?
Income, family, living situation, job, physical condition

What are you doing now that supports this vision?

What are you doing now that stands in the way of this vision?

How do you sabotage yourself?

List your TOP 10 priorities --- do they line up with the vision that you have for your life in 5 years? If not, what must change??

What would you do if you couldn't fail?

If you were a Superhero what would your name be? What would your superpower be?

What is your legacy?
Are you living like that???

What do people remember about you?

In 2020, I give myself permission to:

Who do you want to be when you grow up?

Why?

How can you be more like that NOW?

My biggest fear is_____

What I really want to do is _____

If I could make a living doing whatever I wanted, I would _____

I like people who _____

My favorite thing in the world is _____

What would you like to
- BE

- DO

- HAVE

What's stopping you????

What would you tell your 20-year-old self?

What's your WORD for 2020?

What are the 5 things that you appreciate MOST about yourself?

What historic script is running you right now, underneath everything?

Examples: "money doesn't grow on trees"

"you are not good enough, thin enough, pretty enough, smart enough"

"you can't do it"

"life is hard"

CREATE 2020

Based on what you have revealed to yourself by doing the work in this book, write your new script for 2020. A collection of statements that describe in detail the life that you intend to have in 2020.

Write "as if" these things are already made manifest—

Such as: "I wake up every morning alert and enthusiastic, I take on the day with joy. I am in perfect health making plenty of money and enjoying time with friends and my children... etc.

READ YOUR NEW SCRIPT. EVERY. SINGLE. DAY.

SCRIPT:

Daily Prescription for Changing the Game...
- Bookend your days
- Gratitude Journal Daily
- Review your lists...manifestation, elimination, gratitude –update these lists every 30 days
- Review your vision board or image book or treasure map
- Read your new script
- Spend 30 minutes a day reading, watching or listening to something that forwards the action of your life

Monthly:
- Review this workbook to see that you are on track
- Update your lists and your script if needed

***Suggested...
- Grab a Changing the Game partner to hold you accountable to your practice

Here are some Daily Sheet Templates that can help you bookend your days:

- https://theworkingsinglemom.com/wp-content/uploads/2018/04/daily.pdf
- https://theworkingsinglemom.com/wp-content/uploads/2018/04/weekly.pdf
- https://theworkingsinglemom.com/wp-content/uploads/2018/04/WSM-The-Daily-Plan.pdf

Manifestation list, Gratitude List and Elimination List. You can find them here:

- https://theworkingsinglemom.com/wp-content/uploads/2018/10/TWSM-Manifestation-List.pdf
- https://theworkingsinglemom.com/wp-content/uploads/2018/10/TWSM-Gratitude-List.pdf
- https://theworkingsinglemom.com/wp-content/uploads/2018/10/TWSM-Elimination-List.pdf

ABOUT THE AUTHOR:

Noelle Federico is the owner of Fortunato Partners, Inc., a boutique consulting firm. She is also a social media influencer and the creator of The Working Single Mom brand which has a reach of 24 million people monthly. She writes, teaches, speaks, consults and coaches. Previously she spent 14 plus years as CFO, CMO and Business Manager of Dreamstime.com LLC, where she was a member of the founding team that created the global stock photography leader. Her focus has now returned to corporate training and consulting, writing, coaching and project management. She spends a fair amount of time these days doing Project Management for the Bryn Law Group in Miami, FL.

Noelle has over 35 years of experience in all aspects of business management, finance and development as well as media relations, sales and marketing. She teaches Branding and Marketing and is the author of 'Notes on Branding' and several other books including 'Practical Change... 8 Ways to Rejuvenate Your Life' and 'Practical Change...Inspiration for Kicking Ass & Slaying Dragons. She is also the Founder of the non-profit, A Generous Heart, Inc.

Noelle graduated from Fisher College in Boston, MA and also attended Suffolk University. Additionally, she is a graduate of the Dale Carnegie Training and a Landmark Worldwide graduate.

Formerly of Boston/ Cape Cod, MA and Franklin, TN... she now resides in Fairfax, Vermont to be closer to her parents. She lives with her fiancé, John, her teenage son, Antonio, two large cats and one small cat.

She is always happy to hear from you, and you can always email her at: noelle@fortunatopartners.com

and you can find her here:

https://theworkingsinglemom.com/
https://www.facebook.com/thewrkingsinglemom/
https://twitter.com/wrkingsinglemom
https://www.instagram.com/wrkingsinglemom/
https://www.pinterest.com/wrkingsinglemom/
https://www.linkedin.com/in/noelle-federico-413b5413/
https://www.youtube.com/channel/UCrzzyjoZzGklhInsRb4flpg?reload=9
http://www.revealingexcellence.com/
https://www.facebook.com/revealingexcellence/

MORE BOOKS BY:

One11 Publishing

Practical Change
Inspiration for Kicking Ass & Slaying Dragons!

GetUp Living
Helping Yourself & Others Rise Through Life With Purpose

How Did I Let This Happen?
5 Steps To Help You Move On

Unconditional Forgiveness
Lessons on Letting Go To Build Better Relationships

Unpack Now
Get Rid of the BAGGAGE in Your Relationships

Visit www.one11publishing.com to be inspired!